Be

In the Pocket

Music
Publishing
101

George Howard

Berklee Media

Vice President: Dave Kusek
Dean of Continuing Education: Debbie Cavalier
Director of Business Affairs: Rob Green
Technology Manager: Mike Serio
Marketing Manager, Berkleemusic: Barry Kelly
Senior Graphic Designer: David Ehlers

Berklee Press

Senior Writer/Editor: Jonathan Feist
Senior Writer/Editor: Susan Gedutis Lindsay
Production Manager: Shawn Girsberger
Marketing Manager, Berklee Press: Jennifer Rassler
Product Marketing Manager: David Goldberg

ISBN 0-87639-062-9

1140 Boylston Street
Boston, MA 02215-3693 USA
(617) 747-2146

Visit Berklee Press Online at
www.berkleepress.com

DISTRIBUTED BY

HAL•LEONARD®
CORPORATION
7777 W. BLUEMOUND RD. P.O. BOX 13819
MILWAUKEE, WISCONSIN 53213

Visit Hal Leonard Online at
www.halleonard.com

Printed in the United States of America by Patterson Printing

12 11 10 09 08 07 06 05   5 4 3 2 1

Contents

Introduction

Publishing means presenting something to the "public," generally for a price. When you create something—a song, a photograph, a poem, an invention, etc.—you are legally entitled to part of any money generated from its sale, unless you transfer that right to someone else. This legal protection is called your *copyright*. As soon as you write down or record an original piece of music, you are the exclusive copyright holder of that work.

For this system to work, and for you to make money from a song, various administrative tasks must be completed. You need to officially show that you are the song's creator, set mechanisms in place that ensure you will get paid whenever your song is used, and then convince others to use the song, in order to generate income.

This guide will clarify the steps needed to address these administrative tasks. It introduces you to many of the organizations that can help you in this process, defines important terms, and provides insights that I hope will help you publish your songs profitably. It also discusses many different types of publishing possibilities, and will lead you to many ways of getting paid for your music.

This guide is designed as a quick reference to understand the landscape of the publishing industry. The details of publishing can be complex. This practical guide will help you on a day-to-day basis, and give you a comprehensive introduction to the essential concepts. Use it as a companion to a more in-depth book, such as Eric Beall's *Making Music Make Money* (Berklee Press, 2003).

I hope you find this guide helpful towards getting your songs heard.

—*George Howard*

1. Streams of Publishing Revenue

The money you get from publishing your music comes from two sources: royalties and synchronization fees

Three Types of Royalties

Royalties are percentages of the money gained from others' use of your copyrighted work. There are three principle types of royalties that can be sources of income to you, as a songwriter:

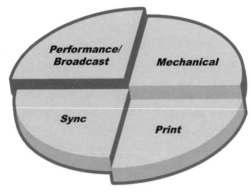

*Note: Not representative of actual percentage

1. **Performance/Broadcast Royalties.** Whenever a song you write is publicly broadcast—such as via the radio or on television, played over a restaurant sound system, or shown in a movie theater—you are entitled to receive a royalty.

2. **Mechanical Royalties.** Whenever a song you write is reproduced as a recording on a CD, cassette, vinyl, or MP3, the person or company that releases that album must pay you, the songwriter, a mechanical royalty.

    Note that this is different and distinct from the "artist" or "record" royalty that a record label pays to the performer of the song on the CD, whether that performer wrote the song or not. If you write and perform the song on a CD, you are entitled to *two* royalties: a mechanical royalty and an artist/record royalty.

3. **Printed Music.** If a song you write is published as sheet music, either alone or in a collection of songs (called a "folio"), you are paid a royalty from the publisher who printed the music.

Synchronization Fees

Synchronization fees are less complicated. These are typically one-time payments in which the producers of a movie, television show, or advertisement will pay you, the songwriter, for the right to include your music in their production. However, once this production is broadcast publicly (on TV, or in a movie, for example), you are then also eligible to receive broadcast royalties.

Let's look at each type of publishing revenue individually.

2. Performance Royalties

Immediately, you should affiliate with one of the *performance rights organizations* (PROs). These organizations keep track of public broadcasts of your music on radio stations, television stations, movie theaters, clubs, restaurants, and other venues. They make sure that you, the songwriter, get paid for these broadcasts.

In order for the PRO to pay you, you must affiliate with one of the three main organizations: ASCAP, BMI, or SESAC. Once you affiliate with one of these PROs, you will fill out forms that list all of the songs you have written and had, or will have, commercially released. The PRO is then able to track the use of your songs in these public places, collect money from users on your behalf, and then compensate you.

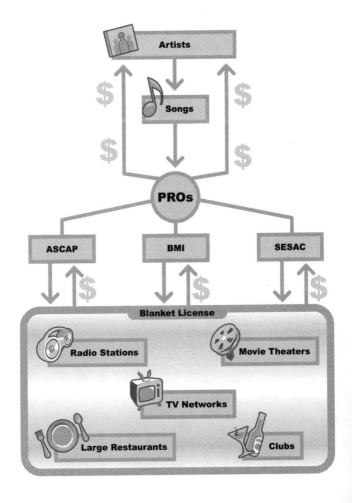

Registering with a PRO, therefore, is your first critical step towards getting paid for the songs you write. It integrates you into the system.

PROs issue blanket licenses to music users—such as television and radio stations, auditoriums, larger restaurants and clubs, hotels, or theme parks—anyone who plays music in a public manner. By paying the blanket license fees to the PROs, these music users are able to use whatever music they want without having to account to each individual songwriter. The blanket license fee's amount is based on broadcast reach; a large commercial radio station pays a higher blanket license fee than a small bookstore, but both pay.

The PROs keep track of the music that is being used through playlists at radio stations, "cue sheets" on television, and by sampling, for other types of users—such as polling restaurants and bars to determine what music they are playing. They pay royalties to writers based on the number of times an affiliated songwriter's music is used. You register with one of the PROs so that they will be able to find you and send you performance royalty checks.

The affiliation processes is easy. There may be an inexpensive, one-time affiliation fee, but once you're affiliated, there is no cost to register as many songs as you write. Check out each PRO, choose one, and affiliate. They all do the same thing, as far as getting you paid goes, and neither is better than the other two, though their additional benefits and services vary.

Contact information for the three performance rights organizations is listed in "Resources," at the end of this book.

Note that PROs are not publishers. Registering with them does not mean you have a publishing deal. PROs simply monitor the public use of copyrights and facilitate royalty payment for these uses.

3. Mechanical Royalties

The mechanical license is crucially important. Stripped of all its rather confusing language and rules, it simply ensures that if a song is released on a recording (i.e., *mechanically reproduced*), the writer of that song will get paid.

Notice that term, mechanical *license*. "License" implies that users of the song—record labels who use the song on one of the CDs they release, for example—do not own the song. Rather, the songwriter is granting them a license to use the song on a record. The label must pay the songwriter for this license.

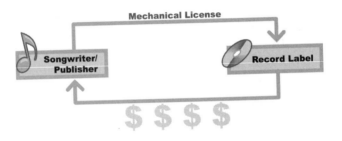

The mechanical license defines what that payment will be and sets rules for when the payments must be made.

The mechanical license protects your single most important asset: your songs. It establishes some guarantees for you that must be met by anyone who wants to use your songs on a record.

Compulsory Licenses

In order to understand mechanical licenses, you must first understand compulsory licenses. A *compulsory license*, as its name suggests, is a license that a songwriter—once certain conditions are met—*must* grant to anyone who wishes to use his song. You read that right: must grant. For instance, if you want to record a version of "Stairway to Heaven" on your own record, you don't have to get anyone's permission to do so. Because of the compulsory license law, you can record anyone's song that has been commercially released and put it on your record, and the writer (or publisher) of that song *must* grant you the license to do so.

However, this compulsory license law also establishes certain guidelines to ensure that songwriters are compensated in a fair and timely manner when their songs are used on other performers' recordings.

Rules of Compulsory Licenses

Here's how it works. You may record someone else's song on your own record if:

1. It has already been commercially released on a record.

2. You pay the song's copyright holder (the writer and/or publisher) a fee—a mechanical royalty based on the "statutory rate." That rate is currently 8.5¢, for songs under five minutes long. It increases periodically.

3. You pay this fee for every recording you manufacture on a fixed medium (such as CD, cassette, or vinyl), whether you sell the recordings or give them away for promotion, etc.

4. You pay 8.5¢ per song. So, if you use four songs by the same writer, you must pay 34¢ per CD made.

5. You pay the copyright holder of this song every month.

If these rules sound a bit harsh, put the shoe on the other foot. When someone uses one of your songs on their album, think of how it benefits you to have them held to the above standards.

The only way around these compulsory license laws is to negotiate a "rate" with the copyright holder to change some of the above terms. Should the copyright holder not want to negotiate with you, you must adhere to the rules. Record labels almost always negotiate a rate with publishers and/or songwriters to avoid paying the full 8.5¢ per song, as well as some of the other more odious requirements, such as paying the publisher/songwriter every month. (Typically, labels pay only 75 percent of this compulsory statutory rate. Usually, they account twice a year.)

Though the compulsory license law is rarely followed to the letter, it still sets the critical guidelines that keep the system flowing. Additionally, just because it is rarely used doesn't mean that it can't be. If you really, really want to record a version of someone else's song, and they won't negotiate a rate with you, you can still record it. You just have to adhere to the rules of the compulsory license law. The law is intended to keep songwriters and publishers from monopolizing their songs.

As a songwriter, you *must* understand how mechanical and compulsory licenses work. They will affect you every time you have a song on a record, whether you perform the song or someone else covers one of your songs. Either way, you are entitled to money from the label that releases the record. It is often the only money that songwriters ever see.

4. Printed Music

If your songs are printed individually as *sheet music*, in a collection of various artists' songs as *folios*, or as a collection of songs from a specific album in a *matching folio*, you are entitled to receive a royalty from the sheet music publisher.

For sheet music, songwriters are paid a royalty—typically 20 percent of the retail price.

For folios, the total royalty is around 10 percent of the retail price, divided among all the contributing songwriters. Each receives a pro-rated share of this royalty based on the number of songs they have included in this folio. For instance, if you have two songs in a ten-song folio, you will receive a fifth of the 10-percent royalty, or a 2-percent royalty of the total retail price.

While printed music is a way for songwriters to make money from their songs, this kind of publishing generally only occurs after you've had some real success. It is not usually relevant to songwriters who are just starting out.

5. Synchronizations

Sync (or "synch" — either way, pronounced "sink") is short for "synchronization." Synchronizations are hugely important in the music business.

Any time music is used in a movie, television show, or commercial, it is referred to as a *sync* (unless it's the theme music). Originally, the term was used for music that was synchronized to moving images in a film, but the term is now used as a catchall.

Whenever music is used in this manner, the producer must pay a fee to the writer/publisher of the music. This is *not* a royalty, such as we have seen above. Rather, it is typically a one-time payment.

Fees for these usages are all over the map. They depend mainly on how successful you are and how much of the song is being used (and how important the song is to the scene). While the fees for songs used on records are established by a compulsory or negotiated mechanical license rate, *there are no such compulsory licensing guidelines for songs used in movies, television shows, or ads.* The producers must negotiate with the songwriter or publisher, who can charge whatever they can get or simply deny usage. Additionally, if the requested song is from a record released by a label, the producer must get permission from and, usually, compensate the label, as well. This is called the "master usage."

Exposure from Syncs

The main benefit from syncs is often not the money. Instead, as radio has become very narrow in its scope, a lot of new music is first heard in movies, television shows, or ads. This exposure can result in significant record sales, and may even lead to record deals. Therefore, syncs can indirectly increase your mechanical royalties.

Producers are certainly hip to the benefits of this exposure for the songwriters, and therefore, will often offer little money for the right to use your music (sometimes none — as is frequently the case with MTV, which is frequently granted the rights to broadcast songs in exchange for "promotional" value; in other words, they don't pay). In these cases, you must weigh whether the exposure is worth giving your copyright away for free.

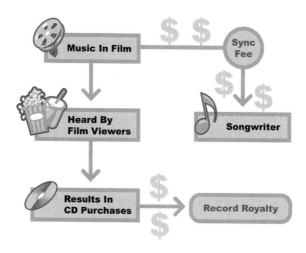

Syncs and Performance Royalties

While the money (a "sync fee") paid to a songwriter for the use of their music in a movie, television show, or ad is typically a one-time payment made by the production's producer, it is not the only income that the songwriter will generate. Because these productions are broadcast publicly, they will generate performance royalties, as well. When that show or movie or ad that has your song in it is broadcast publicly — be it on television, in a movie theater, or over the radio — the broadcasters (not the producers) have to pay a royalty to the songwriter. As we have seen, it is not feasible for these broadcasters to pay to every writer individually. Therefore, they pay a blanket license fee to the PROs (ASCAP, BMI, and SESAC), and then the PROs monitor these broadcasters and distribute royalties — based on the frequency of broadcast — to their affiliated writers.

When your song is used in a television show or ad, you get paid at least twice: once in the form of sync fees, and again in the form of royalties. And if the song is used in a network (not cable) television show, for example, and the show is repeated, you will receive additional performance royalties distributed to you by your PRO.

6. Copyright Registration

Now that you understand the various sources of revenue that can be generated from your songs, you need to also understand how to register your songs and make money from them.

As soon as you commit a song to a fixed, tangible medium, you automatically are the owner of its copyright. Once you record it or write it down, you are the exclusive and sole copyright holder. And this "tangible medium" doesn't have to be fancy. Singing into a boom box or writing out its lyrics, chords, and melody is fine.

You don't *have* to register it, and you certainly don't have to mail it to yourself. But let's look at why songwriters often do so.

One reason is "co-writes." If you write songs with someone else—perhaps you write the music and someone else writes the lyrics, for example—you need to determine between yourselves how to split up the copyright. Maybe, you'll split it 50/50, or maybe you'll decide that one of you should get a larger share.

In the eyes of the law, a song that is jointly composed (no matter who does what) is jointly owned, 50/50, unless otherwise explicitly defined. Establish the breakdown as soon as possible in the songwriting process, in order to avoid problems once the money starts rolling in.

Reasons to Register

Although simply fixing a song in a tangible form does, in fact, establish you as the owner of its copyright, there are very good reasons to take a few extra steps to register your songs, as shown in the Copyright Registration Checklist below.

Most important, registering provides evidence of date of creation, should there ever be an ownership dispute. For instance, say that you write a song and then someone else claims to have written that same song. This person has recorded a version of the song and mailed it to himself, in order to establish the date of creation. If you completed the steps outlined below to register your song, you would likely prevail in the dispute. This is because, in the eyes of the law, registration with the Library of Congress is a more compelling argument for ownership than mailing something to yourself, which can be forged with relative ease. Registration gives you protection and proof in cases of dispute, nothing more.

Every time you finish writing a song, complete these registration tasks. Put a copy of this page where you can see it whenever you write.

Copyright Registration Checklist

❑ **Register the copyright with the U.S. Copyright Office.**

❑ **Send a copy of your song to the Library of Congress.** You can include this with your registration form.

> Library of Congress
> Copyright Office
> 101 Independence Avenue, S.E.
> Washington, D.C. 20559-6000
> (202) 707-3000
> www.loc.gov/copyright/

❑ **Register your song with your PRO.**

ASCAP	BMI	SESAC
One Lincoln Plaza	320 West 57th Street	55 Music Square East
New York, NY 10023	New York, NY 10019-3790	Nashville, TN 37203
212-621-6000	212-586-2000	615-320-0055
www.ascap.com	www.bmi.com	www.sesac.com

This checklist will ensure that you have very good protection, should a dispute arise. Also, by registering with your PRO, it ensures that when your song is publicly broadcast, it can be tracked, and you will be paid.

You can register a group of songs, rather than each song individually, by sending several songs on the same CD. However, you must fill out the forms for each song.

When Copyrights Take Effect

As soon as you either write your song down and/or record it, you automatically hold the copyright to it. Copyrighting your songs gives you certain exclusive rights, such as the right to perform, license, and sell the song. It does not, however, protect you from disputes that may arise from someone else who claims to have written the same song. To protect yourself in case of a dispute, you need to register all of your songs with the U.S. Copyright Office. Mailing a cassette or CD to yourself isn't good enough.

How Long Do Copyrights Last?

The Sonny Bono law, enacted in 1998, states that a copyright can be enforced for the life of the author plus seventy years after death. After this time, the copyright goes into the public domain, and no one can claim copyright ownership.

Using Samples

Sampling—using excerpts from other artists' works—is an increasingly important part of the music business.

Any time you use any piece of sound from someone else's record, you are sampling, and you must "clear" the sample. If you do not, you are violating the copyright laws—using another artist's work without compensating them. It doesn't matter how short the music you take is, how much you alter it, or anything else. It must be cleared.

Clearing Samples

In order to use a sample legally, you must get permission and negotiate a fee with both the song's copyright holder (the writer/publisher) and the record company that released the record from which you are sampling.

Like synchronizations, there are no compulsory license laws when it comes to sampling. Either of these parties can simply say "no." Most, however, will make a deal, but the master holder (the record company, usually) and/or the writer/publisher of the song can charge whatever they think they can get from you.

Further, it is frequently not as cheap or easy as paying these parties and being done with it. Instead, initial payments are usually followed by royalties, based on sales of the song in which the sample is used. By sampling a work, you are essentially dividing the copyright of your work with the people who control the work you sampled from. In most cases, the more "important" or significant the sample is to your new track, the more of the copyright you will give up. If the sample really makes the song, you may end up giving up 100 percent of the copyright, depending on how well you negotiate. So, be careful with your samples.

Replays

Some artists think that if they find a piece of music from another artist's record that they like but don't want to go through the effort and expense of clearing the sample, that they can just re-record this part. Doing this is called a "replay."

A replay does allow you to avoid having to make a deal with the record company for the use of material from a master they own, but you still must make a deal with the writer/publisher of the song you are re-recording. So, while this route is easier by half than a straight sample, it's still not without its complications and costs.

7. Publishers

Why Publishers Exist: Three Roles

With all of this talk of registration and negotiation of licenses, you may be scratching your head and saying, "I just want to write songs, not deal with all of this administrative stuff!"

Well, my friend, you have just articulated the precise reason why publishers exist. Publishers take care of all those "non-creative" details of songwriting. There are three essential tasks, often referred to as "copyright maintenance," that publishers engage in:

1. Registration

2. Exploitation

3. Collection

Of course, they don't do all of this for free. Below, we'll look at these functions and the costs involved.

Registration includes ensuring that your copyrights are registered with the U.S. Copyright Office, that a copy has been sent to the Library of Congress, and that the appropriate forms have been filled out with your PRO to ensure that you collect income from public performances of your music. It also includes granting the appropriate mechanical licenses—be they to record labels or anyone else that wants to use one of your songs on their albums.

None of these registration tasks are terribly difficult. The forms are straightforward, and as long as you are organized and diligent, you should have no problem with the registration.

Exploitation is the process of getting a song used. The word "exploitation" has only positive connotations in the copyrighting business. As a musician, you want your music exploited as much as possible.

Exploiting a copyright effectively is fairly tricky, and it is my belief that a publisher's most significant function is to exploit your music.

There are many ways in which songs can be exploited. The strength of a publisher is in how effective and creative they are at exploiting their copyrights to generate the maximum amount of income for the other copyright holders.

Songwriting Income Streams

Here are some of the many ways that songs can be used.

- On records (via a record deal, if you don't have one already)

- By other artists using your songs, in the form of covers, on their records

- In movies, television, or ads (syncs)

- In sheet music, in the form of folios, etc.

- As ring tones for cell phones

- In video games

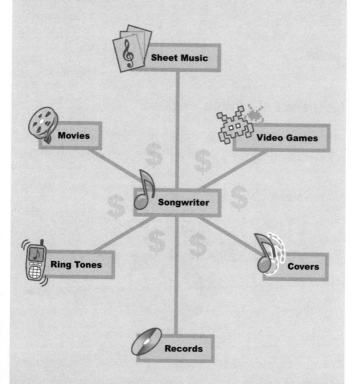

The list goes on and on, and an effective publisher should explore them all. Your publisher needs to be "creative" when it comes to getting your songs into the marketplace.

Collection is the process of getting the songwriter paid. Like registration, collection isn't rocket science, and many artists just do it themselves.

Still, there is something to be said for the leverage that a big publisher can exert when it comes to getting money out of people who are reluctant to pay. You must determine whether this leverage is worth relinquishing some of your earnings.

Why Sign to a Publisher?

Sign with a publisher only if you feel that it can do things that you cannot do on your own. Registration and collection are generally fairly easy, and you may be able to do them on your own. (Beall's *Making Music Make Money* has some good tips for organizing the process.) This really only leaves exploitation. Therefore, in order for you to justify giving up some of your income to a publisher, in my opinion, they darn well better be able to exploit.

Some publishers do not exploit; they only register and collect. These types of publishers may be fine for you if you can exploit yourself, but look closely at how much of your income they are taking to do a job that you could likely do yourself.

Mechanics of a Publishing Deal

Should you determine that you want to enter into a publishing deal, you will have a few (very few) options.

Standard Songwriter Agreement

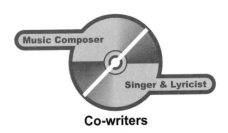

Co-writers

The most typical deal—simply called a "publishing deal" or a "standard songwriter agreement"—is one in which you assign to a publisher 50 percent of the copyrights to your songs written during the term of the deal. The publisher then essentially becomes the co-writer and co-owner of these songs and is entitled to 50 percent of the income that these songs generate, forever—even after the term of the publishing deal has ended. In return, it does all of the things we have mentioned above: register, exploit, and collect.

Co-Writing and PROs

PROs pay the writer's share of income directly to the writer and bypass the publisher. They then pay the publisher's share, which may be divided should you have a co-publishing deal.

Printed music is accounted for slightly differently (and in a more complex manner) than a straight 50/50 split of income.

Co-Publishing Deals

As writers realize they can do many of the things that publishers have typically done, more and more of them are setting up their own publishing companies, and then partnering with a more established publisher to help them. These deals, in which there is more than one publisher, are called *co-publishing deals*. In these deals, the splits between the writer and the publisher are different than 50/50, simply because there is—in theory—more than one publisher involved. For instance, if you set up a publishing company that collects 100 percent of your income, and then you do a deal with another publishing company so that they might help you do a better job, you might only allocate them 20 percent of the income from the copyrights; you keep the other 80 percent.

Similarly, if there is more than one writer for a song, and both have different publishers, a co-publishing deal must be struck between the different publishers, and agreements must be made on, among other things, how the money will be divided.

Some writers avoid this kind of deal because publishers, by taking reduced shares, will tend to work harder for the writers with whom they have straight (rather than "co-") publishing deals.

Publishing Advances

The other major reason for writers opting for straight publishing deals, over co-publishing deals, is because of *advances*.

Straight publishing deals typically pay writers *advances* — upfront money based on expected sales. These advances are "recouped" (that is, paid back) out of all income that the publisher collects prior to any publishing royalties being paid.

Many artists want the cash and want it now. They are therefore willing to sign over 50 percent of their copyrights, in perpetuity, in order to get some upfront money.

Administration Deals

A variation on this theme is often called an *administration deal*. This type of deal states that the publisher has the right to exploit, register, collect, *and* profit from your songs for a set period of time (anywhere from a couple of years to many years). After this time is up, the songs revert back to the publisher of the songs, which may be you, unless you've assigned it to someone else. The publisher — again, maybe you — may then make another deal or administer the songs on their own.

Under these deals, the administrator takes a commission, usually 10 to 25 percent, of any money that comes in while they are administrating the copyrights. They then pay the rest of the money to the original publisher.

Administration deals can occasionally be more elaborate. For instance, some administrators will want to expand their relationship with a writer if they secure a sync or facilitate a cover version of a song.

The Harry Fox Agency

The Harry Fox Agency is a variation on the theme of an administrator. This organization issues mechanical licenses on behalf of the writer or publisher to any label that wants to use them. Additionally, it collects mechanical royalties from these users. The agency takes a 6-percent commission for its services. This is a viable option for even a writer with only a few songs. Do not, however, confuse an agent like the Harry Fox Agency with a publisher. The Harry Fox Agency issues mechanical licenses and collects mechanical royalties, but does not work on behalf of writers. It doesn't exploit the copyrights like a publisher or administrator does. (Contact information for the Harry Fox Agency is provided in the "Resources" section, at the end of this book.)

8. Mechanicals and Record Labels

Typically, songwriters who also perform their own songs on records are likely to be offered big publishing deals when they are about to be signed by a major label. This is because the publisher knows that there will be a record released and therefore mechanical royalties will be paid from the label to the songwriter. Publishers are therefore only too happy to sign performers who also write their own songs, because they know that as soon as the record is released, a stream of income from the labels, in the form of mechanical royalties, will be forthcoming.

The dirty little secret of this otherwise beautiful relationship is that labels have found a way to pay songwriter/performers *less* than what they pay those songwriters who do *not* perform the songs.

Hang in there for details; it's a tricky topic, but very important for songwriters who also perform their own songs and aspire to sign to a label.

Royalties Paid By Labels

When a record label releases a record, it is obligated to pay two different types of royalties:

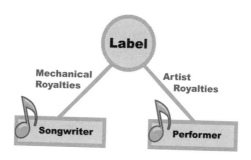

1. Record or Artist Royalties. These are paid to the artist who is signed to the label and performs the songs on the record, whether this person wrote the songs or not. These royalties are typically a percentage of the list price of the album, minus certain deductions and recoupable costs (e.g., packaging, money for tour support, etc.). So, for instance, if you sign to a label and receive a

15-percent royalty, in theory, you receive 15 percent of the list price of the CD, less any contractual deductions after you have sold enough records to become "recouped."

2. Mechanical Royalties. The label pays these to the songs' copyright holder (typically the writer or the writer's publisher), whether or not the writer performs the songs on the album. As we have seen, the amount of this royalty is established by the compulsory mechanical license rate.

Mechanical Royalty Payments

When a record label releases an album, while it may own the album itself and has the right to sell the album forever, it doesn't own the songs on it. Rather, the label is granted a mechanical license from the songwriter or songwriter's publisher to put the songs on their record. In exchange for this license to mechanically reproduce these songs on a CD, the label pays the songwriter or the songwriter's publisher a mechanical royalty. The label must pay this mechanical license every time it sells a copy of this album, for however long the album is in print—or until the song falls into the public domain (seventy years after the death of the songwriter).

This may seem odd, in an era when most people who write their songs also perform them. But fifty years ago, it was very unusual for the performer of the song to also write the song. Frank Sinatra, for example, didn't write any of his songs. The writers (or copyright holders) of all of those great Sinatra songs were paid by Sinatra's label in the form of mechanical royalties, while Sinatra himself was paid by the record label in the form of artist royalties—a percentage of the list price of the record.

This detail is, unfortunately, lost on many artists and is the source of many problems. As a songwriter, you must understand how this process works. Mechanical royalties—money paid to you by your label for the right to put your songs on their records—will frequently be the only money you ever receive from labels.

Controlled Composition Clause

In virtually every contract between a label and an artist, there is something called the *controlled composition clause*. This clause affects you, the songwriter, dramatically, when it comes to the money you receive for your mechanical royalties. In essence, the controlled composition clause is a sort of forced negotiation between the label and the copyright holder of the song being used.

As discussed in "Compulsory Mechanical Licenses," the only way around adhering to the rather strict rules of the compulsory license is for the user (in this case, the record label) to negotiate with the copyright holder.

When Is a Composition "Controlled?"

A song is deemed a *controlled composition* when the signed artist who performs it is also the writer or co-writer, or otherwise stands to gain financially from the copyright. In that case, the label is no longer obligated to adhere to the compulsory mechanical license.

The rationale behind this is that, unlike record royalties, which are paid to performers only after certain costs are recouped, mechanical royalties must be paid to copyright holders from "record one." Many records never recoup their costs, and since it is the labels who end up losing money, they attempt to minimize the amount of money being paid out—hence, the controlled composition clause.

How Controlled Compositions Reduce Your Royalties

In practice, this means that the label is able to reduce the amount of money it pays its artists in mechanical royalties. Here's how:

1. Labels pay only 75 percent of the statutory rate. So, instead of paying 8.5¢ per song, they only pay 6.4¢ on controlled compositions (75 percent of 8.5¢ is 6.4¢).

2. Even if your song is more than five minutes long, labels will only pay you the minimum amount due. That is, they will pay you as if the song was under five minutes.

3. Labels will only pay you on ten songs per album (sometimes eleven). If you release a record with twenty tracks on it, they "cap" the amount of songs they pay on to ten.

4. They will only pay you for records sold, as opposed to records manufactured. This means no payment on promotional CDs.

5. Labels will "fix" or "set" the rate at the time the contract is signed or the record is released. That rate is what they will pay forever, even after the rate goes up.

6. Labels will take any money they owe for non-controlled compositions out of your share. In other words, if you put a cover song on your record, the label will reduce the amount of mechanicals you receive to pay the copyright holder of the cover.

Writer's Royalty Income (Four CD Scenarios)				
	CD 1	CD 2	CD 3	CD 4
Number of Your Originals	1	10	15	15
Number of Covers				1
Actual Income/ Unit Sold	6.4¢	64¢	64¢	55.5¢

(Scenario 4 assumes that the covered songwriter would not negotiate a rate lower than 8.5¢.)

As you can see, this is a tough business. Of course, these are general rules, and the more successful you become, the more leverage you will have in negotiating some of these terms. After you sell a million records, you will likely be able to go back to the label and demand 85 percent of the statutory rate on twelve songs. You'll probably get it ... but only after you've sold a *lot* of records. Largely, these terms are non-negotiable.

Summary

As music moves away from tangible means of distribution and into the digital realm, and as radio continues to narrow its scope, publishing is becoming more and more crucial. The songwriter and/or copyright holder will always get paid, no matter how that song is used or distributed.

Additionally, as record labels are shifting from being distributors to being marketers, once again, the role of the songwriter will become more and more valuable. Songs used in movies, television, and ads are exposed to the biggest audiences, and generate the most significant revenue. Royalties from these placements will continue to be the most significant stream of revenue for most recording artists who write their own songs.

Ultimately, the music industry always has and always will revolve around the song. Taking advantage of this requires an understanding of copyright and publishing. My hope is that this guide helps you along the way.

Resources

ASCAP
One Lincoln Plaza
New York, NY 10023
212-621-6000

www.ascap.com

Berkleemusic.com/Berklee Press
Berklee College of Music
1140 Boylston Street
Boston, MA 02215

www.berkleemusic.com

BMI
320 West 57th Street
New York, NY 10019-3790
212-586-2000

www.bmi.com

The Harry Fox Agency
711 Third Avenue
New York, NY 10017
212-370-5330

www.harryfox.com

SESAC
55 Music Square East
Nashville, TN 37203
615-320-0055

www.sesac.com

U.S. Copyright Office
Library of Congress
101 Independence Ave. S.E.
Washington, D.C. 20559-6000
(202) 707-3000

www.loc.gov/copyright/

Beall, Eric. *Making Music Make Money: An Insider's Guide to the Publishing Industry.* Boston: Berklee Press, 2003.

Glossary

Administration—In publishing, the registration, collection, and exploitation of copyrights.

Administration Deals—Frequently used to refer to publishing deals that are shorter than the life of copyright.

ASCAP—American Society of Composers, Authors, and Publishers. One of the three main performance rights organizations (PROs).

BMI—Broadcast Music Incorporated. One of the three main performance rights organizations.

CMRRA—Canadian Mechanical Rights Reproduction Agency. Canadian counterpart to the Harry Fox Agency.

Co-Publishing Deals—Publishing deals between two or more publishers.

Compulsory License—License that—if certain criteria are met—allows for any song to be re-recorded (covered).

Controlled Composition Clause—Clause in record label contracts that limits the amount of mechanical royalty money labels must pay to writer performers signed to the label.

©—Symbol used in copyright notices, typically found on records, followed by a year. It represents ownership of art and any text on the package itself.

Copyright—Protects "original works of authorship" and grants the holder the right to reproduce, sell, perform, and make a derivative work.

Cover Recording—A recording of a composition that the performing artist did not write.

Cue Sheet—List kept by TV stations, which tracks every musical composition used (and how they are used in the program). Cue sheets are submitted to the PROs, who use them to calculate TV performance royalties for their writers.

First Use—The owner of a song's copyright determines who uses the song first. Once it's been used (recorded and commercially distributed), it can then be "covered" by anyone.

Harry Fox Agency—Issues mechanical licenses for publishers. Collects mechanical income from users for publishers.

Mechanical—The license fee paid by the record label to the writer of the song for the right to "mechanically" reproduce the writer's copyrighted material.

℗ —On a record, this symbol represents a sound recording copyright. It is the copyright of the actual song.

Public Domain (PD)—Songs whose copyright has lapsed. These songs can be recorded and performed by anyone with no royalties due to the writer.

Recoupment—The recovery of expenses by publishers and labels, which are collected before they must pay artist royalties. It is important to clarify what is recoupable by labels or publishers in your contract.

Royalties—Moneys paid from labels or publishers to artists and/or songwriters.

SESAC—One of the three main performance rights organizations.

Sonny Bono Law—Passed in 1998, this law—officially called the Sonny Bono Copyright Extension Act— extends the life of a copyright to seventy years after the last remaining writer of a song dies.

Statutory Rate—The monetary amount that must be paid, per song, in order to receive a mechanical license, which grants the use a copyrighted composition.

Synchronization—In publishing, typically abbreviated as "sync," this refers to using copyrighted music in a movie, TV show, or ad.

Works for Hire—If you get paid to write a song as a "work for hire," when you deliver that song, you have no further claim over it. In fact, the person who commissioned you becomes the legal "author" of the song.

About The Author

Producer, songwriter, author, and musician George Howard founded his first independent label, Slow River Records, in 1993. In 1995, Slow River entered into a co-venture with Rykodisc, one of the world's largest independent labels. In 1999, he was made president of Rykodisc and was fortunate to work with a diverse roster of artists and artist catalogs, including Kelly Willis, Robert Cray, Medeski, Martin & Wood, Morphine, Frank Zappa, Pork Tornado, Josh Rouse, Bill Hicks, Richard Buckner, the Tom Tom Club, Catie Curtis, Future Bible Heroes, Sophie B. Hawkins, and the Slip, among others. He has produced records for many artists, including Kelly Joe Phelps, Chuck E. Weiss (with Tom Waits), Jess Klein, Matthew, and Peter Bruntnell. He recently founded Essex River Works, a music production, marketing, and publishing company. He teaches about the recording industry at Berkleemusic.com and Northeastern University and is a frequent lecturer at Berklee College of Music and many other colleges.

George is author of *Getting Signed: An Insider's Guide to the Record Industry* (Boston: Berklee Press, 2003).